PRESENTED TO:

....

FROM:

....

DATE:

....

BE THE CHANGE

A LISTS & IDEAS JOURNAL
to Help You Shine Your Light for Jesus

JoAnne Simmons

SHILOH kidz
An Imprint of Barbour Publishing, Inc.

Our mission is to inspire the world with the life-changing message of the Bible.

Member of the
Evangelical Christian
Publishers Association

Be THE CHANGe!

You may be young, but that doesn't mean you can't be a mighty big world-changer. You can start right now by doing what God's Word calls you to do—be a shining light! Point others to Jesus and what it means to be a Christian with your faith and loving actions and the way you live your life.

Let this journal help inspire you to spread hope, love, and joy all around you. Start by turning the page and taking the quiz to help you begin to understand how God might use you and your unique gifts. Then go out every day and *be the change* the world needs!

Let no one show little respect for you because you
are young. Show other Christians how to live by your
life. They should be able to follow you in the way
you talk and in what you do. Show them how
to live in faith and in love and in holy living.
1 TIMOTHY 4:12

Our bodies are made up of many parts.
None of these parts have the same use.
There are many people who belong to Christ.
And yet, we are one body which is Christ's.
We are all different but we depend on each other.
We all have different gifts that God
has given to us by His loving-favor.
We are to use them. If someone has the gift of
preaching the Good News, he should preach.
He should use the faith God has given him.
If someone has the gift of helping others,
then he should help.
If someone has the gift of teaching, he should teach.
If someone has the gift of speaking words of
comfort and help, he should speak.
If someone has the gift of sharing what
he has, he should give from a willing heart.
If someone has the gift of leading other
people, he should lead them.
If someone has the gift of showing kindness
to others, he should be happy as he does it.

ROMANS 12:4–8

DISCOVERING MY GIFTS QUIZ

✹ For each statement in the quiz, choose one of the following responses and write the number next to the statement.

__1__ Nope. Never.

__2__ Hardly ever.

__3__ Sorta, kinda, sometimes.

__4__ Yes, a lot.

__5__ Totally! All the time!

✹ Add up your numbers in each category and put the total next to the spiritual gift.

✹ Circle the top scores to find your strongest spiritual gifts. Then use them to *be the change*!

__3__ (P) I see things very clearly as right or wrong.

__4__ (S) I love to make and do things with my hands, and I'm good at it.

__3__ (T) It makes me so happy to learn new things and read and study on my own.

__3__ (E) Many people say I am happy, fun, and easy to talk to.

__4__ (G) I like to create cool gifts to give to others.

__5__ (L) I love meeting goals, getting projects done, and accomplishing new things.

__3__ (M) I feel very sad and angry when bad things happen to people.

_3_ (P) I'm not afraid to speak openly and honestly with others, even about difficult things.

_5_ (S) Helping others makes me very happy.

_4_ (T) I think it's fun to teach people about things they didn't know before.

_5_ (E) I like to focus on the positives in life.

_3_ (G) I like to use my imagination and think up creative ways to give to people in need.

_5_ (L) I always want to win a game or competition. I want to be the best at everything I do.

_3_ (M) I don't enjoy playing in competitive sports.

_1_ (P) I like to follow rules, and I get frustrated when others break the rules.

_4_ (S) I am shy and easily embarrassed.

_3_ (T) I'm good at talking to others and sharing my thoughts and ideas clearly.

_5_ (E) It's easy for me to notice what people can do well, and I like to tell them.

_3_ (G) I do everything with great enthusiasm and joy.

_3_ (L) I have lots of confidence in front of other people.

_4_ (M) I like to look for the good in people rather than the bad.

_5_ (P) I love God's Word, and I sense God speaking to me and leading me in many different ways.

_4_ (S) I don't ever like to say no when people ask for my help.

_5_ (T) I don't mind doing things on my own. I like to be independent.

_3_ (E) I get along well with most people, and I enjoy listening and talking to them.

_5_ (G) Giving money or needed items to others makes me feel very happy.

__3__ (L) I enjoy taking charge, telling people what to do, and organizing tasks when I'm working in a group.

__5__ (M) I prefer peace and try hard to avoid conflict.

Total = __15__ for (P) statements:

Prophecy/Perceiving – You are very sensitive to and good at listening to God, and you want to share His message with others.

Total = __17__ for (S) statements:

Serving – You are practical, and you love to support good causes and help others in need, often behind the scenes.

Total = __15__ for (T) statements:

Teaching – You are full of knowledge and great at constantly learning and teaching others what you have learned.

Total = __16__ for (E) statements:

Encouraging – You are hopeful and great at encouraging others and helping them discover what's good for them.

Total = __14__ for (G) statements:

Giving – You are generous and good at saving money and items and coming up with new ideas to help others who are in need.

Total = __16__ for (L) statements:

Leadership – You are confident and responsible and able to see a goal and direct others toward achieving that goal.

Total = __15__ for (M) statements:

Mercy – You are compassionate and easily feel the loving heart of God toward others.

Do your results on the "Discovering My Gifts" quiz seem like they match up with what you think about yourself and your abilities? Do they match up with what wise people have told you about yourself and your abilities? Why or why not?

....

....

....

....

....

....

....

....

....

....

....

....

....

....

....

God has given each of you a gift. Use it to help
each other. This will show God's loving-favor.
1 PETER 4:10

BE THE CHANGE

✳ I can pray for God to show me exactly who, how, and where to start helping others today.

✳ I can use my gifts and abilities to help others.

✳ Things I enjoy doing that help others and match up with my gifts are:

✳ ....

✳ ....

✳ ....

✳ ....

✳ ....

✳ ....

✳ ....

✳ ....

✳ ....

✳ ....

✳ ....

✳ ....

✳ ....

✳ ....

When does your light shine brightest for Jesus? Describe a specific time you remember sharing God's hope and love (and maybe you even did it without saying anything about God's hope and love).

Let your light shine. . . . Then [others] will see the good
things you do and will honor your Father Who is in heaven.
MATTHEW 5:16

Be the CHANGE

�֍ I can light the world around me by sharing God's hope and love.

✷ I can generously give light to others so that they too may have light to share.

✷ ....

✷ ....

✷ ....

✷ ....

✷ ....

✷ ....

✷ ....

✷ ....

✷ ....

✷ ....

✷ ....

✷ ....

✷ ....

✷ ....

✷ ....

✷ ....

What is the difference between just working and working *for Jesus*?

We are His work. He has made us to belong to Christ Jesus
so we can work for Him. He planned that we should do this.

EPHESIANS 2:10

BE THE CHANGE

✸ Everything I do can be done in a way that honors and serves Jesus.

✸ I can pray and sing praise to God in my mind, no matter what task I'm doing.

✸ ....

✸ ....

✸ ....

✸ ....

✸ ....

✸ ....

✸ ....

✸ ....

✸ ....

✸ ....

✸ ....

✸ ....

✸ ....

✸ ....

✸ ....

Think about your mom, dad, or other wise and trustworthy grown-ups in your life.
How can they help teach and inspire you to be the change in the world around you?

Remember your leaders who first spoke God's Word to you.
Think of how they lived, and trust God as they did.
HEBREWS 13:7

BE THE CHANGE

✷ I can ask wise grown-ups in my life to help direct me where to be the change.

✷ I can pray to always have good mentors in my life.

✷ ....

✷ ....

✷ ....

✷ ....

✷ ....

✷ ....

✷ ....

✷ ....

✷ ....

✷ ....

✷ ....

✷ ....

✷ ....

✷ ....

The closest place to be the change is in your own home. How does loving, respecting, and obeying your parents at home help you be the change in the world?

Children, obey your parents in everything. The Lord is pleased when you do.
COLOSSIANS 3:20

BE THE CHANGE

✴ I can obey my parents, even when I really don't feel like it.

✴ I can respect and have a good attitude toward my parents, even if I don't always understand or agree with them.

✴ I can surprise my parents by doing helpful things around the house without even being asked!

✴ ....

✴ ....

✴ ....

✴ ....

✴ ....

✴ ....

✴ ....

✴ ....

✴ ....

✴ ....

✴ ....

✴ ....

✴ ....

✴ ....

What are your responsibilities around your home and with your family? When you do them well, how do you think that helps you be the change in the world?

Anyone who does not take care of his family
and those in his house has turned away from the faith.
1 TIMOTHY 5:8

BE THE CHANGE

✻ I can do my chores around the house with a good attitude.

✻ I can strive to get along well with my parents and siblings—and have fun with them!

✻ ....

✻ ....

✻ ....

✻ ....

✻ ....

✻ ....

✻ ....

✻ ....

✻ ....

✻ ....

✻ ....

✻ ....

✻ ....

✻ ....

✻ ....

✻ ....

✻ ....

Do you have siblings? Are they younger or older? Do you have good relationships with them now, or do you need to work on making good changes in your relationships with them?

....

....

....

....

....

....

....

....

....

....

....

....

....

....

Be sure your love is true love. Hate what is sinful. Hold on to whatever is good. Love each other as Christian brothers. Show respect for each other.

ROMANS 12:9-10

BE THE CHANGE

✳ I can work on good relationships with my siblings.

✳ I can pray for my siblings and my relationships with them.

✳ I can show love and forgiveness to my siblings—even when they drive me crazy!

✳ ....

✳ ....

✳ ....

✳ ....

✳ ....

✳ ....

✳ ....

✳ ....

✳ ....

✳ ....

✳ ....

✳ ....

✳ ....

✳ ....

✳ ....

✳ ....

How do you think good relationships with your siblings helps you be the change in the world?

....

....

....

....

....

....

....

....

....

....

....

....

....

....

Put out of your life all these things: bad feelings about other people, anger, temper, loud talk, bad talk which hurts other people, and bad feelings which hurt other people. You must be kind to each other. Think of the other person. Forgive other people just as God forgave you because of Christ's death on the cross.

EPHESIANS 4:31–32

Be THe CHANGe

- I can choose good and kind words to say to my siblings.
- I can share my stuff with my siblings.
- I can find ways to play well and enjoy time with my siblings.

Who are your neighbors to whom you can show kindness and love? Imagine a world where every person reached out to help take care of the people who live right next to them. Describe what that would be like.

....

....

....

....

....

....

....

....

....

....

....

....

....

....

"I give you a new Law. You are to love each other. You must love
each other as I have loved you. If you love each other,
all men will know you are My followers."

JOHN 13:34–35

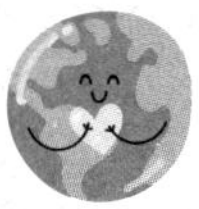

Be The Change

- I can pray for my neighbors.
- I can spend time with a neighbor who is lonely.

Where do you go to school? What do you love about your school? What are the things that could use improvement in your school?

An understanding mind gets much learning,
and the ear of the wise listens for much learning.
PROVERBS 18:15

BE THE CHANGE

* ✳ I can look for things that need improvement in my school.
* ✳ I can pray and ask God to show me how I could help with those things.
* ✳ I can ask trusted teachers and leaders in my school how I can help with these problems.

✳ ....

✳ ....

✳ ....

✳ ....

✳ ....

✳ ....

✳ ....

✳ ....

✳ ....

✳ ....

✳ ....

✳ ....

✳ ....

✳ ....

What is your attitude toward going to school, doing your work, and listening to your teachers? How do you think your attitudes in those things can affect others around you?

....

....

....

....

....

....

....

....

....

....

....

....

....

....

....

....

Whatever you say or do, do it in the name of the Lord Jesus.
Give thanks to God the Father through the Lord Jesus.
COLOSSIANS 3:17

Be THe CHANGe

- ✹ I can choose good attitudes about schoolwork and homework.
- ✹ I can listen and obey teachers and leaders in my school.
- ✹ My good behavior at school can help other students want to have good behavior at school too.

✹ ....

✹ ....

✹ ....

✹ ....

✹ ....

✹ ....

✹ ....

✹ ....

✹ ....

✹ ....

✹ ....

✹ ....

✹ ....

✹ ....

✹ ....

Think about your closest friends. What do you like best about them and what do you love to do together? Why are they your close friends?

A friend loves at all times.
PROVERBS 17:17

Be THe CHANGe

✴ I can thank my friends when they are kind to me and share with me.

✴ I can ask my friends how I can pray for them.

✴ I can share and show love to my friends, and that encourages us all to do more good things for one another!

✴ ....

✴ ....

✴ ....

✴ ....

✴ ....

✴ ....

✴ ....

✴ ....

✴ ....

✴ ....

✴ ....

✴ ....

✴ ....

✴ ....

✴ ....

Think about the kids who frustrate you at school. What about their behavior is so frustrating? What do you think some of the causes of their behavior might be?

_____

_____

_____

_____

_____

_____

_____

_____

_____

_____

_____

_____

_____

_____

_____

Most of all, have a true love for each other.
Love covers many sins.
1 PETER 4:8

Be the Change

✳ I can pray for the difficult kids at school.

✳ I can show kindness and love to the difficult kids at school.

✳ I can reach out to the kids who look lonely at school.

✳ ....

✳ ....

✳ ....

✳ ....

✳ ....

✳ ....

✳ ....

✳ ....

✳ ....

✳ ....

✳ ....

✳ ....

✳ ....

✳ ....

✳ ....

Do you know kids at your school with special needs and special abilities? What are ways you see others helping them and how could you join in?

....

....

....

....

....

....

....

....

....

....

....

....

....

....

....

....

God has chosen you. You are holy and loved by Him. Because of this,
your new life should be full of loving-pity. You should be kind
to others and have no pride. Be gentle and be willing to
wait for others. Try to understand other people.

COLOSSIANS 3:12-13

Be the Change

✳ I can pray for people with special needs and special abilities.

✳ I don't ever have to be afraid of people with special needs and special abilities.

✳ I can talk to people with special needs and special abilities and their caregivers to get to know them better and become a friend to them.

✳ ....

✳ ....

✳ ....

✳ ....

✳ ....

✳ ....

✳ ....

✳ ....

✳ ....

✳ ....

✳ ....

✳ ....

✳ ....

✳ ....

Think about the people you know with special needs and their helpers. How can you let them encourage and inspire you?

Help each other in troubles and problems.
This is the kind of law Christ asks us to obey.
GALATIANS 6:2

Be the Change

✳ I can be on the lookout for people in wheelchairs and hold the door open for them if needed.

✳ I can be quiet and gentle with people who are sensitive to loud noises, bright lights, big crowds, and things like that.

✳ I can be kind to people with food allergies and help keep the foods they're allergic to away from them.

✳ ....

✳ ....

✳ ....

✳ ....

✳ ....

✳ ....

✳ ....

✳ ....

✳ ....

✳ ....

✳ ....

✳ ....

✳ ....

✳ ....

Who are your favorite teachers and leaders at school? What do you think it's like to have their jobs?

....

....

....

....

....

....

....

....

....

....

....

....

....

....

Those who do right do not have to be afraid of the leaders.
Those who do wrong are afraid of them. Do you want to be
free from fear of them? Then do what is right. You will be
respected instead. Leaders are God's servants to help you.

ROMANS 13:3–4

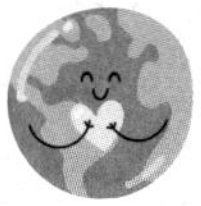

Be the Change

- I can show respect to my teachers and leaders at school.
- I can pray for all the teachers, leaders, and staff at school.
- I can write notes to encourage my teachers.

What kinds of things make you sad? Do you sometimes see sadness in others?
What makes you sense they are sad?

_____

_____

_____

_____

_____

_____

_____

_____

_____

_____

_____

_____

_____

We give thanks to the God and Father of our Lord Jesus Christ. He is our
Father Who shows us loving-kindness and our God Who gives us comfort.
He gives us comfort in all our troubles. Then we can comfort other people
who have the same troubles. We give the same kind of comfort
God gives us. As we have suffered much for Christ and have
shared in His pain, we also share His great comfort.

2 CORINTHIANS 1:3-5

BE THE CHANGE

✳ I can pray and ask God to show me when people around me are sad.

✳ I can ask God to help me understand how to cheer them up.

✳ ....

✳ ....

✳ ....

✳ ....

✳ ....

✳ ....

✳ ....

✳ ....

✳ ....

✳ ....

✳ ....

✳ ....

✳ ....

✳ ....

✳ ....

✳ ....

What are your favorite sports? How can being involved in sports help you be the change in the world?

....

....

....

....

....

....

....

....

....

....

....

....

....

....

Keep yourself growing in God-like living. Growing strong in body is all right but growing in God-like living is more important. It will not only help you in this life now but in the next life also. These words are true and they can be trusted. Because of this, we work hard and do our best because our hope is in the living God, the One Who would save all men. He saves those who believe in Him.

1 TIMOTHY 4:7-10

Be the Change

✶ I can respect and show kindness and teamwork to my coaches and teammates.

✶ I can encourage teammates when we lose a game or competition.

✶ I can show good sportsmanship when winning a game or competition.

✶ ....

✶ ....

✶ ....

✶ ....

✶ ....

✶ ....

✶ ....

✶ ....

✶ ....

✶ ....

✶ ....

✶ ....

✶ ....

Describe the last time you were sick. What helped make you feel better?

....

....

....

....

....

....

....

....

....

....

....

....

....

....

....

....

Dear friend, I pray that you are doing well in every way.
I pray that your body is strong and well even as your soul is.
3 JOHN 1:2

Be THE CHANGe

✱ I can pray for people I know who are sick.

✱ I can help them by doing or suggesting the kinds of things that make me feel better when I'm sick.

✱ ....

✱ ....

✱ ....

✱ ....

✱ ....

✱ ....

✱ ....

✱ ....

✱ ....

✱ ....

✱ ....

✱ ....

✱ ....

✱ ....

✱ ....

✱ ....

Try to imagine what it must be like to be homeless. Describe how you think you would feel. What would you do and where would you go?

He who shows kindness to a poor man gives to the Lord
and He will pay him in return for his good act.
PROVERBS 19:17

BE THE CHANGE

✻ I can pray for those in my community and the world who are poor and needy.

✻ I can donate items to shelters and organizations that help homeless and needy people.

✻ ....

✻ ....

✻ ....

✻ ....

✻ ....

✻ ....

✻ ....

✻ ....

✻ ....

✻ ....

✻ ....

✻ ....

✻ ....

✻ ....

Have you encountered people who treat others badly because of the way they look or their skin color? How did that make you feel? How would you feel if you were treated that way?

....

....

....

....

....

....

....

....

....

....

....

....

....

....

....

*"The Lord does not look at the things man looks at. A man looks
at the outside of a person, but the Lord looks at the heart."*
1 SAMUEL 16:7

Be the Change

✻ I can remember that God made and loves all people the same because He looks at the heart, not the outward appearance.

✻ I can ask for God's help to see people as He does and love them like He does.

✻ I can choose to show kindness and love to others who are being mistreated because of the way they look.

✻ ....

✻ ....

✻ ....

✻ ....

✻ ....

✻ ....

✻ ....

✻ ....

✻ ....

✻ ....

✻ ....

✻ ....

✻ ....

✻ ....

Who are some of the elderly people in your life? Why should you listen to them and learn from them?

_____

_____

_____

_____

_____

_____

_____

_____

_____

_____

_____

_____

_____

_____

_____

Hair that is turning white is like a crown of honor.
It is found in the way of being right with God.
PROVERBS 16:31

Be the Change

- ✵ I can show love and respect for elderly people.
- ✵ I can visit elderly people in nursing homes.
- ✵ I can color pictures and make cards for people in nursing homes.
- ✵ ....
- ✵ ....
- ✵ ....
- ✵ ....
- ✵ ....
- ✵ ....
- ✵ ....
- ✵ ....
- ✵ ....
- ✵ ....
- ✵ ....
- ✵ ....
- ✵ ....
- ✵ ....
- ✵ ....

Describe activities, such as dance or art classes or soccer, that you're involved in. What do you love about them?

We all have different gifts that God has given to us
by His loving-favor. We are to use them.
ROMANS 12:6

BE THE CHANGE

✸ I can encourage someone who is struggling to get the dance routine memorized.

✸ I can cheerfully help clean up a messy spill in art class.

✸ I can cheer on my teammates—even when they're having a rough game.

✸ ....

✸ ....

✸ ....

✸ ....

✸ ....

✸ ....

✸ ....

✸ ....

✸ ....

✸ ....

✸ ....

✸ ....

✸ ....

✸ ....

Have you ever lost a loved one? What helped you in your sadness? How do you honor and remember that loved one?

The Lord is near to those who have a broken heart.
And He saves those who are broken in spirit.

Psalm 34:18

Be the Change

✱ I can pray for people I know who have lost loved ones.

✱ I can send a card to encourage someone I know who has recently lost a loved one.

✱ ....

✱ ....

✱ ....

✱ ....

✱ ....

✱ ....

✱ ....

✱ ....

✱ ....

✱ ....

✱ ....

✱ ....

✱ ....

✱ ....

✱ ....

✱ ....

Do you enjoy going to the library and reading? What are your favorite books?

A wise man will hear and grow in learning. A man of understanding
will become able to understand a saying and a picture-story,
the words of the wise and what they mean.
PROVERBS 1:5-6

Be the Change

- ✴ I can follow the rules in the library.
- ✴ I can write a librarian a thank-you note for helping me find good books.

✴ ....

✴ ....

✴ ....

✴ ....

✴ ....

✴ ....

✴ ....

✴ ....

✴ ....

✴ ....

✴ ....

✴ ....

✴ ....

✴ ....

✴ ....

✴ ....

Describe the neighborhood where you live. What do you love best about it? In what ways could it be better?

_____

_____

_____

_____

_____

_____

_____

_____

_____

_____

_____

_____

_____

_____

_____

_____

Live this free life by loving and helping others. You obey the whole Law
when you do this one thing, "Love your neighbor as you love yourself."
GALATIANS 5:13-14

BE THE CHANGE

✻ I can offer to babysit or play with younger kids in my neighbor-hood to help their parents.

✻ I can offer to help do yardwork for a neighbor who is struggling to get it done.

✻ ....

✻ ....

✻ ....

✻ ....

✻ ....

✻ ....

✻ ....

✻ ....

✻ ....

✻ ....

✻ ....

✻ ....

✻ ....

✻ ....

✻ ....

Do you visit any elderly or special-needs family or friends in a nursing home? How does it make you feel when you visit them?

My body and my heart may grow weak,
but God is the strength of my heart and all I need forever.
PSALM 73:26

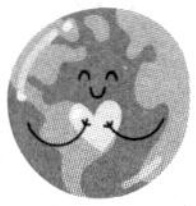

Be THE CHANGE

- I can pray for people in nursing homes.
- I can cheerfully visit people in nursing homes.
- I can encourage my sports teams and activity groups to visit nursing homes together.

What do you think it's like to work at a nursing home?

_____

_____

_____

_____

_____

_____

_____

_____

_____

_____

_____

_____

_____

_____

This is the reason we do not give up. Our human body is wearing out.
But our spirits are getting stronger every day. The little troubles
we suffer now for a short time are making us ready for
the great things God is going to give us forever.
2 CORINTHIANS 4:16-17

Be THE CHANGE

✷ I can pray for caregivers and staff at nursing homes.

✷ I can encourage caregivers and staff at nursing homes by thanking them for what they do.

✷ I can ask caregivers and staff at nursing homes if there are other things I can do to help.

✷ ....

✷ ....

✷ ....

✷ ....

✷ ....

✷ ....

✷ ....

✷ ....

✷ ....

✷ ....

✷ ....

✷ ....

✷ ....

✷ ....

Where do you go to church? What do you love about your church?

....

....

....

....

....

....

....

....

....

....

....

....

....

....

....

Let us hold on to the hope we say we have and not be changed. We can
trust God that He will do what He promised. Let us help each other to love
others and to do good. Let us not stay away from church meetings.
HEBREWS 10:23-25

Be the Change

✴ I can pray for God to bless and help my church.

✴ I can go to church regularly and be ready and eager to learn.

✴ I can serve at my church.

✴ ....

✴ ....

✴ ....

✴ ....

✴ ....

✴ ....

✴ ....

✴ ....

✴ ....

✴ ....

✴ ....

✴ ....

✴ ....

✴ ....

✴ ....

✴ ....

Who are the pastors and leaders and teachers at church? What do you admire about them?

....

....

....

....

....

....

....

....

....

....

....

....

....

....

Christ gave gifts to men. He gave to some the gift to be missionaries, some to be preachers, others to be preachers who go from town to town. He gave others the gift to be church leaders and teachers. These gifts help His people work well for Him. And then the church which is the body of Christ will be made strong.

EPHESIANS 4:11–12

Be the Change

✳ I can pray for the pastors, leaders, teachers, and staff at my church.

✳ I can thank and encourage the pastors, leaders, teachers, and staff at my church.

✳ ....

✳ ....

✳ ....

✳ ....

✳ ....

✳ ....

✳ ....

✳ ....

✳ ....

✳ ....

✳ ....

✳ ....

✳ ....

✳ ....

Write down the lyrics to your favorite worship songs. Why are they your favorites?

Keep on teaching and helping each other. Sing the Songs of David and the church songs and the songs of heaven with hearts full of thanks to God.

COLOSSIANS 3:16

Be the Change

✭ I can sing worship songs anytime, anywhere, out loud or even just in my mind.

✭ I can share worship songs with others who need encouragement.

✭ ....

✭ ....

✭ ....

✭ ....

✭ ....

✭ ....

✭ ....

✭ ....

✭ ....

✭ ....

✭ ....

✭ ....

✭ ....

✭ ....

✭ ....

✭ ....

Describe your favorite park or playground. Why is it your favorite?

Be full of joy always because you belong to the Lord.
Again I say, be full of joy!
PHILIPPIANS 4:4

Be the Change

✷ After a rainy day, I can take a towel to the park and dry off all the slides and swings.

✷ When playing with other kids at the playground, I can give up my swing so someone else can have a turn.

✷ I can play with younger kids and help watch out for them.

✷ ....

✷ ....

✷ ....

✷ ....

✷ ....

✷ ....

✷ ....

✷ ....

✷ ....

✷ ....

✷ ....

✷ ....

✷ ....

✷ ....

What makes you feel stressed or anxious? Do you sometimes see that in others? How do you know they are stressed or anxious?

You are standing under the powerful hand of God. At the right time He will lift you up. Give all your worries to Him because He cares for you.

1 Peter 5:6-7

Be THe CHANGe

✴ I can pray and ask God to show me people who are stressed or anxious.

✴ I can ask God to know how to help them calm down.

✴ I can pray with people who are stressed or anxious.

✴ ....

✴ ....

✴ ....

✴ ....

✴ ....

✴ ....

✴ ....

✴ ....

✴ ....

✴ ....

✴ ....

✴ ....

✴ ....

✴ ....

✴ ....

Would you ever want to serve in the military when you're grown up? Why or why not? What do you think it's like to serve in the military?

....

....

....

....

....

....

....

....

....

....

....

....

....

....

....

Will You not go out with our armies, O God? O give us help
against those who hate us. For the help of man is worth nothing.
With God's help we will do great things. And He will break
under His feet those who fight against us.

PSALM 108:11–13

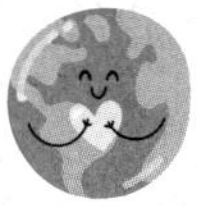

Be the Change

- I can pray for people in all branches of the military.
- I can thank and encourage people who serve in the military for helping give me freedom and for protecting our nation.

Do you have any loved ones in the military, or do you know any friends who have loved ones in the military? How does that feel?

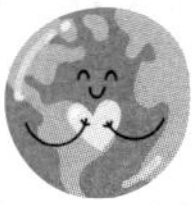

Be the Change

- I can pray specifically for loved ones in the military.
- I can send cards and letters and treats to encourage people I know in the military.

What are your favorite foods? Imagine and describe what it might feel like if your family didn't have enough food to eat.

....

....

....

....

....

....

....

....

....

....

....

....

....

....

....

What if a Christian does not have clothes or food? And one of you
says to him, "Goodbye, keep yourself warm and eat well." But if
you do not give him what he needs, how does that help
him? A faith that does not do things is a dead faith.

JAMES 2:15–17

Be the Change

✴ I can be grateful for what I do have and give thanks to God.

✴ I can pray for those who are needy and ask God to show me how to help them.

✴ I can collect and donate canned goods to local food banks to help the hungry.

✴ ....

✴ ....

✴ ....

✴ ....

✴ ....

✴ ....

✴ ....

✴ ....

✴ ....

✴ ....

✴ ....

✴ ....

✴ ....

What is your favorite movie? Why is it your favorite?

....

....

....

....

....

....

....

....

....

....

....

....

....

....

....

....

*"We must remember what the Lord Jesus said,
'We are more happy when we give than when we receive.'"*
ACTS 20:35

BE THE CHANGE

✸ I can ask God for wisdom in choosing to watch movies that are good for me.

✸ I can plan a movie night to encourage my friends.

✸ I can help make snacks to share for the movie night.

✸ ....

✸ ....

✸ ....

✸ ....

✸ ....

✸ ....

✸ ....

✸ ....

✸ ....

✸ ....

✸ ....

✸ ....

✸ ....

✸ ....

What do you think is most beautiful about God's Creation? Why?

_____

_____

_____

_____

_____

_____

_____

_____

_____

_____

_____

_____

_____

_____

_____

"Our Lord and our God, it is right for You to have the shining-
greatness and the honor and the power. You made all things."

REVELATION 4:11

BE THE CHANGE

✻ I can pick up trash when I see it to help keep God's beautiful creation clean.

✻ I can help recycle.

✻ I can try not to waste water and electricity.

✻ ....

✻ ....

✻ ....

✻ ....

✻ ....

✻ ....

✻ ....

✻ ....

✻ ....

✻ ....

✻ ....

✻ ....

✻ ....

✻ ....

What is your favorite store to shop at? Why is it your favorite?

"Give, and it will be given to you. You will have more than enough. It can be pushed down and shaken together and it will still run over as it is given to you. The way you give to others is the way you will receive in return."

LUKE 6:38

BE THE CHANGE

✳ I can be respectful of other shoppers when I'm in a store.

✳ I can offer to return shopping carts in the parking lot.

✳ I can be kind and polite to cashiers.

✳ ....

✳ ....

✳ ....

✳ ....

✳ ....

✳ ....

✳ ....

✳ ....

✳ ....

✳ ....

✳ ....

✳ ....

✳ ....

✳ ....

✳ ....

Would you ever want to be a police officer? Why or why not? What do you think it's like to be a police officer?

....

....

....

....

....

....

....

....

....

....

....

....

....

....

....

Teach your people to obey the leaders of their country. They should be ready to do any good work. They must not speak bad of anyone, and they must not argue. They should be gentle and kind to all people.

Titus 3:1–2

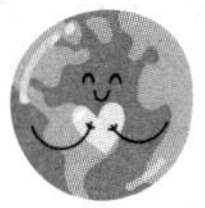

Be The Change

- I can pray for police officers.
- I can thank police officers for doing their job when I see them.
- I can visit my local police station and take cards or treats to encourage police officers.

What were your favorite books and stories when you were younger? Why? How have your reading choices changed as you've grown older?

....

....

....

....

....

....

....

....

....

....

....

....

....

....

....

....

Everything that was written in the Holy Writings long ago was written
to teach us. By not giving up, God's Word gives us strength and hope.
ROMANS 15:4

Be the Change

✻ I can donate old books to libraries or to share with kids in the hospital.

✻ I can leave a little sticky note of encouragement inside each book I donate.

✻ ....

✻ ....

✻ ....

✻ ....

✻ ....

✻ ....

✻ ....

✻ ....

✻ ....

✻ ....

✻ ....

✻ ....

✻ ....

✻ ....

✻ ....

Do you like to cook or help out in the kitchen at home? Why or why not?

So if you eat or drink or whatever you do,
do everything to honor God.
1 CORINTHIANS 10:31

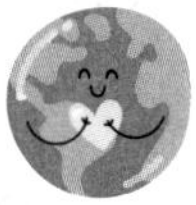

Be the Change

- I can cheerfully help out in the kitchen at home.
- I can learn to cook and bake.
- I can share the food I make with others.

How do you feel about doing your homework? Do you ever feel overwhelmed by it?

Do not let yourselves get tired of doing good. If we do not give up, we will
get what is coming to us at the right time. Because of this, we should do
good to everyone. For sure, we should do good to those who belong to Christ.
GALATIANS 6:9-10

Be THe CHANGe

✷ I can choose to have a good attitude about homework.

✷ I can try to help other classmates and younger siblings with their homework if they need it.

✷ I can organize group study times with classmates to help one another.

✷ ....

✷ ....

✷ ....

✷ ....

✷ ....

✷ ....

✷ ....

✷ ....

✷ ....

✷ ....

✷ ....

✷ ....

✷ ....

✷ ....

Have one of your parents ever experienced the loss of a job? How did that affect your family? How did it make you feel?

....

....

....

....

....

....

....

....

....

....

....

....

....

"Do not worry. Do not keep saying, 'What will we eat?' or, 'What will we drink?' or, 'What will we wear?' The people who do not know God are looking for all these things. Your Father in heaven knows you need all these things. First of all, look for the holy nation of God. Be right with Him. All these other things will be given to you also. Do not worry about tomorrow. Tomorrow will have its own worries. The troubles we have in a day are enough for one day."

MATTHEW 6:31–34

BE THE CHANGE

✻ I can pray for people I know who have just lost a job.

✻ I can encourage and share scripture in Matthew 6 with someone who has lost a job.

✻ ....

✻ ....

✻ ....

✻ ....

✻ ....

✻ ....

✻ ....

✻ ....

✻ ....

✻ ....

✻ ....

✻ ....

✻ ....

✻ ....

What is your favorite restaurant? Why is it your favorite?

A dish of vegetables with love is better than
eating the best meat with hate.

PROVERBS 15:17

BE THE CHANGE

✹ I can use extra good manners when I go out to eat.

✹ I can leave a friendly note with a generous tip for the server.

✹ ....

✹ ....

✹ ....

✹ ....

✹ ....

✹ ....

✹ ....

✹ ....

✹ ....

✹ ....

✹ ....

✹ ....

✹ ....

✹ ....

✹ ....

✹ ....

What kinds of things make you feel angry? Do you sometimes sense anger in others? How do you know they are angry?

He who is slow to anger is better than the powerful.
PROVERBS 16:32

BE THE CHANGE

✻ I can pray and ask God to help me when I feel angry.

✻ I can ask God for wisdom to know how to help others deal with their anger.

✻ ....

✻ ....

✻ ....

✻ ....

✻ ....

✻ ....

✻ ....

✻ ....

✻ ....

✻ ....

✻ ....

✻ ....

✻ ....

✻ ....

✻ ....

What are your favorite things about Christmas? Why do you think people sometimes feel sad during Christmas?

"Joseph, son of David, do not be afraid to take Mary as your wife. She is to become a mother by the Holy Spirit. A Son will be born to her. You will give Him the name Jesus because He will save His people from the punishment of their sins."

MATTHEW 1:20-21

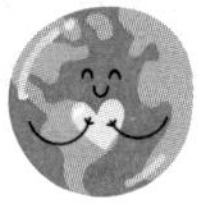

Be the Change

- I can pray and ask God to help me focus on the real meaning of Christmas.
- I can pray for people who feel sad during Christmas.
- I can give simple gifts and help spread love and joy to all around me during Christmas.

Do you know how to sew or make things with wood or would you like to learn?
Why or why not?

_She opens her hand to the poor,
and holds out her hands to those in need._

PROVERBS 31:20

Be the Change

✳ I can learn to sew and do woodwork.

✳ I can use sewing skills to help out others who might need some clothing mended.

✳ I can make a gift for someone with my woodworking abilities.

✳ ....

✳ ....

✳ ....

✳ ....

✳ ....

✳ ....

✳ ....

✳ ....

✳ ....

✳ ....

✳ ....

✳ ....

✳ ....

✳ ....

What does it mean to have common courtesy? Do you think our world has enough of it these days?

....

....

....

....

....

....

....

....

....

....

....

....

....

....

Keep having the same love. Be as one in thoughts and actions.
Nothing should be done because of pride or thinking about yourself.
Think of other people as more important than yourself. Do not
always be thinking about your own plans only. Be happy
to know what other people are doing.
PHILIPPIANS 2:2-4

BE THE CHANGE

✸ I can promote common courtesy with my respect and kindness for others.

✸ I can think of others first, and remember the world does not revolve around me.

✸ ....

✸ ....

✸ ....

✸ ....

✸ ....

✸ ....

✸ ....

✸ ....

✸ ....

✸ ....

✸ ....

✸ ....

✸ ....

✸ ....

✸ ....

Would you ever want to be a doctor, a nurse, or another medical professional when you grow up? Why or why not? What do you think it's like to have those jobs?

A glad heart is good medicine.
PROVERBS 17:22

BE THE CHANGE

✻ I can be grateful for good medical care.

✻ I can pray for doctors, nurses, and other medical professionals.

✻ ....

✻ ....

✻ ....

✻ ....

✻ ....

✻ ....

✻ ....

✻ ....

✻ ....

✻ ....

✻ ....

✻ ....

✻ ....

✻ ....

✻ ....

✻ ....

✻ ....

Have you ever met a missionary and heard his or her stories? What about them inspired you?

_____

_____

_____

_____

_____

_____

_____

_____

_____

_____

_____

_____

_____

_____

_____

"Go and make followers of all the nations. Baptize them in the name
of the Father and of the Son and of the Holy Spirit. Teach them
to do all the things I have told you. And I am with
you always, even to the end of the world."
MATTHEW 28:19–20

Be the Change

- I can pray for full-time missionaries all over the world.
- I can ask my parents and my church leaders how to support full-time missionaries.

Have you ever been on a mission trip? Where did you go and what did you do?

....

....

....

....

....

....

....

....

....

....

....

....

....

....

....

....

"But you will receive power when the Holy Spirit comes into your life.
You will tell about Me in the city of Jerusalem and over all the
countries of Judea and Samaria and to the ends of the earth."

ACTS 1:8

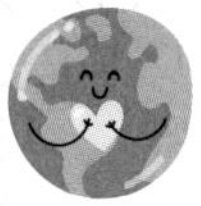

Be the Change

- I can pray and ask God for guidance about going on mission trips.
- I can pray for people I know going on short-term mission trips.

What is your favorite way to celebrate New Year's Eve and New Year's Day? Do you like to make New Year's resolutions?

....

....

....

....

....

....

....

....

....

....

....

....

....

....

....

....

"God will take away all their tears. There will be no more death or sorrow or crying or pain. All the old things have passed away." Then the One sitting on the throne said, "See! I am making all things new."

REVELATION 21:4-5

BE THE CHANGE

✳ I can start a new year with renewed hope and trust in God.

✳ I can make goals to pray and read my Bible every day in the New Year.

✳ I can encourage others to trust God more and pray and read His Word more in the New Year.

✳ ....

✳ ....

✳ ....

✳ ....

✳ ....

✳ ....

✳ ....

✳ ....

✳ ....

✳ ....

✳ ....

✳ ....

✳ ....

✳ ....

Do you enjoy going grocery shopping? Describe what you like or dislike about it.

Go and eat your bread in happiness.
ECCLESIASTES 9:7

Be the Change

✻ At the grocery store, I can happily help the grown-up I'm with.

✻ While waiting in line, I can be patient and kind.

✻ ....

✻ ....

✻ ....

✻ ....

✻ ....

✻ ....

✻ ....

✻ ....

✻ ....

✻ ....

✻ ....

✻ ....

✻ ....

✻ ....

✻ ....

Describe a time when you were left out and excluded by others. How did that make you feel?

....

....

....

....

....

....

....

....

....

....

....

....

....

....

....

....

Remember to do good and help each
other. Gifts like this please God.
HEBREWS 13:16

BE THE CHANGE

✳ I can look for others who seem to be excluded and find ways to include them.

✳ I can encourage my friends to include others in what we're doing or playing.

✳ ....

✳ ....

✳ ....

✳ ....

✳ ....

✳ ....

✳ ....

✳ ....

✳ ....

✳ ....

✳ ....

✳ ....

✳ ....

✳ ....

✳ ....

Do you like to celebrate Valentine's Day? Why or why not?

....

....

....

....

....

....

....

....

....

....

....

....

....

....

....

Dear friends, let us love each other, because love comes from God.
Those who love are God's children and they know God. Those who do not
love do not know God because God is love. God has shown His love to us
by sending His only Son into the world. God did this so we might have life
through Christ. This is love! It is not that we loved God but that He loved
us. For God sent His Son to pay for our sins with His own blood.

1 JOHN 4:7-10

BE THE CHANGE

✵ I can celebrate and spread love because it all comes from God.

✵ I can share scripture to help others know what real love truly is.

✵ ....

✵ ....

✵ ....

✵ ....

✵ ....

✵ ....

✵ ....

✵ ....

✵ ....

✵ ....

✵ ....

✵ ....

✵ ....

✵ ....

Describe a time you felt unimportant because you are younger and smaller than others. Then describe blessings you have experienced because you are younger and smaller.

....

....

....

....

....

....

....

....

....

....

....

....

....

....

....

Let no one show little respect for you because you are young.
Show other Christians how to live by your life. They should be
able to follow you in the way you talk and in what you do.
Show them how to live in faith and in love and in holy living.
1 TIMOTHY 4:12

Be the Change

✴ I can thank God for the age and size I am now.

✴ I can ask God what things I can do to help others while I'm at my current age and size that perhaps they cannot do.

✴ I can use my small size and energy to help people who do not have the abilities and energy that I have, even just fetching things for elderly people who can't walk as easily as I can.

✴ ....

✴ ....

✴ ....

✴ ....

✴ ....

✴ ....

✴ ....

✴ ....

✴ ....

✴ ....

✴ ....

✴ ....

✴ ....

✴ ....

Do you have pets? Describe them and what you love about them.

"But ask the wild animals, and they will teach you. Ask the birds of the
heavens, and let them tell you. Or speak to the earth, and let it teach you.
Let the fish of the sea make it known to you. Who among all these does
not know that the hand of the Lord has done this? In His hand is
the life of every living thing and the breath of all men."

JOB 12:7-10

Be the Change

✴ I can pray and thank God for wonderful animals in His creation!

✴ I can cheerfully help take care of my own pets.

✴ I can check with local animal shelters and ask what I can do to help.

✴ ....

✴ ....

✴ ....

✴ ....

✴ ....

✴ ....

✴ ....

✴ ....

✴ ....

✴ ....

✴ ....

✴ ....

✴ ....

✴ ....

If you have dogs, do you ever take them to the park or to public places? Describe your favorite outing with your dog.

Do for other people what you would
like to have them do for you.
LUKE 6:31

Be The Change

✺ I can check with nursing homes near me to see if I could bring my dog to cheer up elderly people.

✺ I can respect other people who may or may not like dogs when I take my dog in public places.

✺ I can clean up after my dog in public places.

✺ ....

✺ ....

✺ ....

✺ ....

✺ ....

✺ ....

✺ ....

✺ ....

✺ ....

✺ ....

✺ ....

✺ ....

✺ ....

✺ ....

Would you ever want to be a firefighter or rescue worker when you grow up? Why or why not? What do you think it's like to have that kind of job?

I can do all things because Christ gives me the strength.
PHILIPPIANS 4:13

BE THE CHANGE

✻ I can pray for firefighters and rescue workers.

✻ I can thank the firefighters and rescue workers in my community.

✻ ....

✻ ....

✻ ....

✻ ....

✻ ....

✻ ....

✻ ....

✻ ....

✻ ....

✻ ....

✻ ....

✻ ....

✻ ....

✻ ....

✻ ....

What is your favorite way to celebrate your birthday? What do you like about celebrating birthdays of family members and friends?

Your eyes saw me before I was put together. And all the days of my life were written in Your book before any of them came to be.
PSALM 139:16

BE THE CHANGE

✳ I can praise God on my birthday (and every day!) for giving me life and good things He wants me to do.

✳ I can praise God for others on their birthdays too!

✳ ....

✳ ....

✳ ....

✳ ....

✳ ....

✳ ....

✳ ....

✳ ....

✳ ....

✳ ....

✳ ....

✳ ....

✳ ....

✳ ....

✳ ....

Do you know the story about the day you were born? (Ask your parents if you don't already know.) Write it down here.

_____

_____

_____

_____

_____

_____

_____

_____

_____

_____

_____

_____

_____

_____

_____

You put me together inside my mother. I will give thanks to
You, for the greatness of the way I was made brings fear.
Your works are great and my soul knows it very well.
Psalm 139:13–14

Be the Change

✯ I can pray for moms who are expecting babies.

✯ I can ask grown-ups how to help at local pregnancy care centers.

✯ ....

✯ ....

✯ ....

✯ ....

✯ ....

✯ ....

✯ ....

✯ ....

✯ ....

✯ ....

✯ ....

✯ ....

✯ ....

✯ ....

✯ ....

Do you have any friends or family who are adopted? Or maybe you are! What adoption stories do you know? What inspires you about them?

_____

_____

_____

_____

_____

_____

_____

_____

_____

_____

_____

_____

_____

_____

_____

Religion that is pure and good before God the Father is to help children who have no parents and to care for women whose husbands have died who have troubles. Pure religion is also to keep yourself clean from the sinful things of the world.

JAMES 1:27

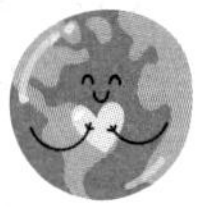

Be the Change

- I can pray for families who have adopted children.
- I can pray for more people to want to adopt orphans.
- I can ask God and grown-ups what I can do to help adoptive families and orphans.

Have you ever been injured or needed surgery or stayed overnight in a hospital? Describe your experience. How did people help you? How did the help make you feel?

....

....

....

....

....

....

....

....

....

....

....

....

....

....

Happy is the man who cares for the poor. The Lord will save him in times of trouble. The Lord will keep him alive and safe. And he will be happy upon the earth. You will not give him over to the desire of those who hate him. The Lord will give him strength on his bed of sickness. When he is sick, You will make him well again.

PSALM 41:1–3

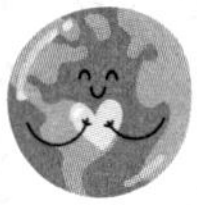

Be the Change

- I can pray for someone I know who is injured or in the hospital.
- I can make and send a card to someone I know who is in the hospital.

Do you know any families who help children in foster care? Or do you know a friend or classmate in foster care? How do you think it must feel to be in foster care?

Jesus said, "Let the little children come to Me. Do not stop them.
The holy nation of heaven is made up of ones like these."
He put His hands on them and went away.
MATTHEW 19:14–15

Be the Change

✻ I can pray for children in foster care and the families who are fostering them.

✻ I can ask grown-ups for help with donating items to a family I know who is fostering kids.

✻ I can offer to help do household chores for a family who is fostering kids.

✻ ....

✻ ....

✻ ....

✻ ....

✻ ....

✻ ....

✻ ....

✻ ....

✻ ....

✻ ....

✻ ....

✻ ....

✻ ....

✻ ....

Do you know there are Christians all over the world in countries where their lives are in danger if they share their faith? What would it feel like to be in the shoes of these persecuted Christians?

You must pray at all times as the Holy Spirit leads you to pray.
Pray for the things that are needed. You must watch and
keep on praying. Remember to pray for all Christians.
EPHESIANS 6:18

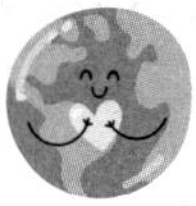

Be the Change

- I can remember to pray regularly for persecuted Christians.
- I can remind others to pray regularly for persecuted Christians.

What do you love best about celebrating Easter?

The angel said to the women, "Do not be afraid. I know you are
looking for Jesus Who was nailed to the cross. He is not here!
He has risen from the dead as He said He would."

MATTHEW 28:5-6

Be the Change

✯ I can help share the good news of Easter, that Jesus is alive!

✯ I can invite people to church for Easter.

✯ ....

✯ ....

✯ ....

✯ ....

✯ ....

✯ ....

✯ ....

✯ ....

✯ ....

✯ ....

✯ ....

✯ ....

✯ ....

✯ ....

✯ ....

Have you ever encountered a bully? What happened?

"Be strong and have strength of heart. Do not be afraid or shake with fear because of them. For the Lord your God is the One Who goes with you. He will be faithful to you. He will not leave you alone."

DEUTERONOMY 31:6

Be the Change

✷ I can pray for bullies to stop being cruel to others.

✷ I can pray for kids being bullied.

✷ I can be brave and stand up to bullies, but also ask grown-ups to help in bullying situations.

✷ ....

✷ ....

✷ ....

✷ ....

✷ ....

✷ ....

✷ ....

✷ ....

✷ ....

✷ ....

✷ ....

✷ ....

✷ ....

✷ ....

✷ ....

Do you enjoy singing or do you play any musical instruments? What is your favorite type of music?

....

....

....

....

....

....

....

....

....

....

....

....

....

....

Come, let us sing with joy to the Lord. Let us sing loud with joy
to the rock Who saves us. Let us come before Him giving
thanks. Let us make a sound of joy to Him with songs.
PSALM 95:1–2

Be The Change

�֍ I can use my talents to give praise to God because they are gifts from Him!

✖ I can practice my talent to keep getting better.

✖ I can ask leaders in my church and community how I can bless others with my musical talents.

✖ ....

✖ ....

✖ ....

✖ ....

✖ ....

✖ ....

✖ ....

✖ ....

✖ ....

✖ ....

✖ ....

✖ ....

✖ ....

✖ ....

Do you have a favorite video game? Why is it your favorite?

Teach young men to be wise. In all things show them how to live by your life and by right teaching.

Titus 2:6-7

Be the CHANGe

✿ I can be careful not to spend too much time on video games.

✿ I can be careful when choosing what types of video games I will play.

✿ ....

✿ ....

✿ ....

✿ ....

✿ ....

✿ ....

✿ ....

✿ ....

✿ ....

✿ ....

✿ ....

✿ ....

✿ ....

✿ ....

✿ ....

Do you know anyone who has a therapy pet or service dog? Or have you seen one in public? What inspires you about them and their owners?

....

....

....

....

....

....

....

....

....

....

....

....

....

....

"If you give what you have to the hungry, and fill the needs of those who suffer, then your light will rise in the darkness, and your darkness will be like the brightest time of day. The Lord will always lead you. He will meet the needs of your soul in the dry times and give strength to your body. You will be like a garden that has enough water, like a well of water that never dries up."

ISAIAH 58:10–11

Be the Change

✷ I can pray for people who have therapy pets and service dogs.

✷ I can be respectful and not touch therapy pets and service dogs unless their owner says it's okay.

✷ ....

✷ ....

✷ ....

✷ ....

✷ ....

✷ ....

✷ ....

✷ ....

✷ ....

✷ ....

✷ ....

✷ ....

✷ ....

✷ ....

✷ ....

How does memorizing Bible verses help you be the change in the world?

All the Holy Writings are God-given and are made alive by Him. Man is helped when he is taught God's Word. It shows what is wrong. It changes the way of a man's life. It shows him how to be right with God. It gives the man who belongs to God everything he needs to work well for Him.

2 TIMOTHY 3:16-17

Be the Change

✫ I can make goals for memorizing scripture.

✫ I can share scripture that I have memorized with others.

✫ ....

✫ ....

✫ ....

✫ ....

✫ ....

✫ ....

✫ ....

✫ ....

✫ ....

✫ ....

✫ ....

✫ ....

✫ ....

✫ ....

✫ ....

✫ ....

What do you love best about Thanksgiving?

Be full of joy all the time. Never stop praying. In everything give thanks.
This is what God wants you to do because of Christ Jesus.
1 Thessalonians 5:16-18

BE THE CHANGE

✸ I can pray for people who might not have family to be with on Thanksgiving.

✸ I can help serve a community Thanksgiving meal.

✸ ....

✸ ....

✸ ....

✸ ....

✸ ....

✸ ....

✸ ....

✸ ....

✸ ....

✸ ....

✸ ....

✸ ....

✸ ....

✸ ....

✸ ....

✸ ....

Do you hear grown-ups talk a lot about politics and government leaders? What interests or confuses you about those topics?

....

....

....

....

....

....

....

....

....

....

....

....

....

....

Obey the head leader of the country and all other leaders over you.
This pleases the Lord. Obey the men who work for them. God sends
them to punish those who do wrong and to show respect to those
who do right. This is what God wants. When you do right,
you stop foolish men from saying bad things.
1 PETER 2:13–15

BE THE CHANGE

- ✳ I can pray for our government leaders.
- ✳ I can treat others with respect even if we disagree about politics.
- ✳ I can send respectful letters to government leaders to both encourage them and ask them to do good things for our communities and our nation.

✳ ....

✳ ....

✳ ....

✳ ....

✳ ....

✳ ....

✳ ....

✳ ....

✳ ....

✳ ....

✳ ....

✳ ....

✳ ....

✳ ....

What season of the year is your favorite? Why is it your favorite?

"While the earth lasts, planting time and gathering time, cold and heat, summer and winter, and day and night will not end."

GENESIS 8:22

Be THE CHANGE

✺ I can help my family get our home ready for each new season.

✺ I can offer to help neighbors get their homes and yards ready for each new season.

✺ ....

✺ ....

✺ ....

✺ ....

✺ ....

✺ ....

✺ ....

✺ ....

✺ ....

✺ ....

✺ ....

✺ ....

✺ ....

✺ ....

✺ ....

✺

Describe the worst argument you've ever had with a sibling or friend. How did you work it out?

My Christian brothers, you know everyone should listen much
and speak little. He should be slow to become angry.

JAMES 1:19

Be the Change

✳ I can ask God for help when I'm arguing with a friend or family member.

✳ I can be quick to say I'm sorry and quick to forgive when I've had a conflict with a friend or family member.

✳ ....

✳ ....

✳ ....

✳ ....

✳ ....

✳ ....

✳ ....

✳ ....

✳ ....

✳ ....

✳ ....

✳ ....

✳ ....

✳ ....

What are your favorite kinds of fruit and why do you like them? What does it mean to have the fruit of the Spirit that the Bible talks about?

....

....

....

....

....

....

....

....

....

....

....

....

....

....

....

The fruit that comes from having the Holy Spirit in our lives is: love, joy, peace, not giving up, being kind, being good, having faith, being gentle, and being the boss over our own desires.
GALATIANS 5:22–23

BE THE CHANGE

✻ I can memorize what the fruits of the Spirit are.

✻ I can ask God to help the fruits of the Spirit grow abundantly in my life.

✻ ....

✻ ....

✻ ....

✻ ....

✻ ....

✻ ....

✻ ....

✻ ....

✻ ....

✻ ....

✻ ....

✻ ....

✻ ....

✻ ....

✻ ....

What does it mean to be a missionary? Do you have to travel to a foreign country to be a missionary?

....

....

....

....

....

....

....

....

....

....

....

....

....

....

Jesus came and said to them, "All power has been given to Me in heaven and on earth. Go and make followers of all the nations. Baptize them in the name of the Father and of the Son and of the Holy Spirit. Teach them to do all the things I have told you. And I am with you always, even to the end of the world."

MATTHEW 28:18–20

Be The Change

✺ I can be a missionary anywhere I am.

✺ I can pray for missionaries all over the world who are helping others come to know Jesus as their Savior.

✺ I can write letters to encourage missionaries.

✺ ....

✺ ....

✺ ....

✺ ....

✺ ....

✺ ....

✺ ....

✺ ....

✺ ....

✺ ....

✺ ....

✺ ....

✺ ....

✺ ....

✺ ....

What are your favorite TV shows? Do you think people watch too much TV these days? Why or why not?

....

....

....

....

....

....

....

....

....

....

....

....

....

....

....

Keep your minds thinking about whatever is true, whatever is respected,
whatever is right, whatever is pure, whatever can be loved,
and whatever is well thought of.

PHILIPPIANS 4:8

Be THE CHANGE

✵ I can be careful to not spend too much time watching TV.

✵ I can be careful with what I choose to watch.

✵ I can pray for wisdom about what and when to watch.

✵ ....

✵ ....

✵ ....

✵ ....

✵ ....

✵ ....

✵ ....

✵ ....

✵ ....

✵ ....

✵ ....

✵ ....

✵ ....

✵ ....

✵ ....

Are you a messy or a neat person? How does taking responsibility for your stuff and your messes help you be the change in the world?

Everyone must do his own work.

GALATIANS 6:5

Be the Change

- I can clean up after myself.
- I can help younger kids learn to pick up after themselves.

Do you enjoy waiting in line? What do you do to help pass the time patiently?

_____

_____

_____

_____

_____

_____

_____

_____

_____

_____

_____

_____

_____

_____

_____

I pray that God's great power will make you strong,
and that you will have joy as you wait and do not give up.
COLOSSIANS 1:11

Be The Change

✳ I can let others go in front of me in line.

✳ I can try to make younger kids smile while waiting in line.

✳ I can carry stickers with me to share with other kids who are also waiting in line.

✳ ....

✳ ....

✳ ....

✳ ....

✳ ....

✳ ....

✳ ....

✳ ....

✳ ....

✳ ....

✳ ....

✳ ....

✳ ....

✳ ....

✳ ....

Do you think you and your friends spend too much time on your phones and social media these days? Why or why not?

....

....

....

....

....

....

....

....

....

....

....

....

....

....

....

....

Teach us to understand how many days we have.
Then we will have a heart of wisdom to give You.
PSALM 90:12

Be the Change

✱ I can pray and ask God for wisdom in using social media.

✱ I can limit my time using social media, and more importantly I can spend time on good friendships and relationships in person.

✱ ....

✱ ....

✱ ....

✱ ....

✱ ....

✱ ....

✱ ....

✱ ....

✱ ....

✱ ....

✱ ....

✱ ....

✱ ....

✱ ....

✱ ....

✱ ....

What are some of your worst fears? How can letting God help you with them also help you be the change in the world?

Give great honor to the Lord with me. Let us praise His name together.
I looked for the Lord, and He answered me. And He took away all my fears.

PSALM 34:3–4

Be The Change

✱ I can ask God for help with my fears, and I can praise Him when I am afraid.

✱ I can focus on His Word and His power and His love for me.

✱ I can help others pray to God and praise Him when they are afraid.

✱ ....

✱ ....

✱ ....

✱ ....

✱ ....

✱ ....

✱ ....

✱ ....

✱ ....

✱ ....

✱ ....

✱ ....

✱ ....

✱ ....

Describe a time when you said something mean you wish you'd never said. How did you work it out? How can controlling your tongue help you be the change in the world?

....

....

....

....

....

....

....

....

....

....

....

....

....

....

....

He who watches over his mouth and his
tongue keeps his soul from troubles.

PROVERBS 21:23

Be the Change

✳ I can ask God for help to control what I say.

✳ I can ask forgiveness when I say the wrong thing.

✳ I can choose to not participate when others are gossiping or saying bad things.

✳ ....

✳ ....

✳ ....

✳ ....

✳ ....

✳ ....

✳ ....

✳ ....

✳ ....

✳ ....

✳ ....

✳ ....

✳ ....

✳ ....

✳ ....

Have you ever been made fun of by other kids? Describe how you felt.

....

....

....

....

....

....

....

....

....

....

....

....

....

....

"In the last days there will be men who will laugh at the truth and will be led by their own sinful desires." They are men who will make trouble by dividing people into groups against each other. Their minds are on the things of the world because they do not have the Holy Spirit. Dear friends, you must become strong in your most holy faith. Let the Holy Spirit lead you as you pray. Keep yourselves in the love of God.

JUDE 1:18-21

Be the CHANGe

✷ I can pray for God's help and wisdom when other kids make fun of me.

✷ I can ask a grown-up for help when other kids make fun of me.

✷ I can refuse to join in when I see kids making fun of someone else.

✷ ....

✷ ....

✷ ....

✷ ....

✷ ....

✷ ....

✷ ....

✷ ....

✷ ....

✷ ....

✷ ....

✷ ....

✷ ....

✷ ....

How is God's wisdom different from the world's wisdom?

If you do not have wisdom, ask God for it. He is always ready
to give it to you and will never say you are wrong for asking.
You must have faith as you ask Him. You must not doubt.

JAMES 1:5-6

Be the Change

✷ I can pray every day for God to give me His wisdom.

✷ I can focus on what the Bible says is right more than what the world says is right.

✷ I can share God's wisdom with others.

✷ ....

✷ ....

✷ ....

✷ ....

✷ ....

✷ ....

✷ ....

✷ ....

✷ ....

✷ ....

✷ ....

✷ ....

✷ ....

✷ ....

Describe a time when you lied and then the lie was discovered. How did you feel?
Or describe a time when you were tempted to lie but decided not to.

We want to do the right thing.
We want God and men to know we are honest.
2 CORINTHIANS 8:21

BE THE CHANGE

✻ I can ask for God's help to be honest in all things, big and small.

✻ I can choose to always tell the truth, even when it's hard, even when I know I'll get in trouble.

✻ ....

✻ ....

✻ ....

✻ ....

✻ ....

✻ ....

✻ ....

✻ ....

✻ ....

✻ ....

✻ ....

✻ ....

✻ ....

✻ ....

✻ ....

✻ ....

Describe times when neighbors have done kind things for your family. How did that encourage and inspire you?

Each of us should live to please his neighbor.
This will help him grow in faith.
ROMANS 15:2

Be the Change

✷ I can help cook and take a meal to my neighbors just because.

✷ I can organize a neighborhood lemonade stand and give all the money earned to charity.

✷ I can draw encouraging messages and chalk art on my neighbors' sidewalks (but I'll check with a grown-up first to make sure it's okay).

✷ ....

✷ ....

✷ ....

✷ ....

✷ ....

✷ ....

✷ ....

✷ ....

✷ ....

✷ ....

✷ ....

✷ ....

✷ ....

✷ ....

✷ ....

How do you keep God first in your life? How does keeping God first in your life help you be the change?

....

....

....

....

....

....

....

....

....

....

....

....

....

....

But even if you suffer for doing what is right, you will be happy.
Do not be afraid or troubled by what they may do to make it hard
for you. Your heart should be holy and set apart for the Lord God.
Always be ready to tell everyone who asks you why you believe
as you do. Be gentle as you speak and show respect.
1 PETER 3:14-15

Be the CHANGE

* I can choose every day to put God first in my life.
* I can make sure I'm making time for daily Bible reading and prayer.
* ....
* ....
* ....
* ....
* ....
* ....
* ....
* ....
* ....
* ....
* ....
* ....
* ....
* ....
* ....
* ....

Have you used this book to help you shine your light for Jesus? Describe some of your experiences.

....

....

....

....

....

....

....

....

....

....

....

....

....

....

....

Jesus sat down and called the followers to Him. He said, "If anyone wants
to be first, he must be last of all. He will be the one to care for all."

MARK 9:35

Be THe CHANGe

✻ I can share my faith with others and invite them to church.

✻ I can be the change the world needs by living my life for Jesus no matter what.

✻ ....

✻ ....

✻ ....

✻ ....

✻ ....

✻ ....

✻ ....

✻ ....

✻ ....

✻ ....

✻ ....

✻ ....

✻ ....

✻ ....

✻ ....

✻ ....

Have you used this journal to help you be the change in the world? Describe some of your results and experiences.

....

....

....

....

....

....

....

....

....

....

....

....

....

We know what love is because Christ gave His life for us. We should give our lives for our brothers. What if a person has enough money to live on and sees his brother in need of food and clothing? If he does not help him, how can the love of God be in him? My children, let us not love with words or in talk only. Let us love by what we do and in truth. This is how we know we are Christians.

1 JOHN 3:16-19

Be the Change

✻   I can be the change wherever I go and whatever I do, with the love of Jesus overflowing from me.

✻   I can inspire others to be the change too.

✻ ....

✻ ....

✻ ....

✻ ....

✻ ....

✻ ....

✻ ....

✻ ....

✻ ....

✻ ....

✻ ....

✻ ....

✻ ....

✻ ....

✻ ....

✻ ....

✻ ....

CONTINUE TO "BE THE CHANGE" WITH. . .

180 Prayers to Change the World

Make a positive impact, wherever you are,
as you pray for positive change in your world.
Each of the 180 prayers will guide you
to talk to God about. . .

your friends
your family
your neighborhood
your school
your city
your country
and more!

You'll see how God works *through you* as you
listen for His voice and direction in your life.

Paperback / 978-1-64352-016-2 / $4.99